# Contents

# CHAPTER 1

# We the People

Everyone likes to belong. We belong to a family, to a group of friends, or, perhaps, to a team. We also belong to a place, and that makes us citizens. We are citizens, first and foremost, of the United States. We are also citizens of the state we live in. Coloradans are citizens of Colorado. You don't have to be a grown-up to be a citizen; even newborn babies are citizens. You can even consider yourself a citizen of your school.

A citizen is a person. (Sorry, dogs, cats, and whistle-pigs!) A citizen is protected by the laws of the country, state, and city. A citizen enjoys certain **privileges**, but also has responsibilities. For example, he or she must obey those laws.

Who says so? The Constitution says so. The United States Constitution is a **legal** document that explains how the nation's **government** works. It also spells out the **rights** and responsibilities of **citizenship**.

The U.S. Constitution was written in 1787. At that time, there were only 13 states, with a combined population of about 4 million people. Colorado was still a wilderness. The eastern part of the state was part of French Louisiana, which stretched from the Gulf of Mexico to Canada.

The famous first words of the Constitution, "We the People of the United States," originally listed each individual state from north to south instead of "the United States."

*The original U.S. Constitution is kept at the National Archives Museum in Washington, D.C. This is the first page of the original four-page document.*

Citizenship means being a citizen; it defines who we are and gives us a sense of identity. A nation—or a state—is more than just some land. A nation is its people. We are the people. The Constitution of the United States begins with these words: "We the People."

## PREAMBLE TO U.S. CONSTITUTION:

We the People of the United States, in Order to form a more perfect Union, establish Justice, insure domestic Tranquility, provide for the common defense, promote the general Welfare, and secure the Blessings of Liberty to ourselves and our Posterity, do ordain and establish this Constitution for the United States of America.

# CHAPTER 2

# The State Constitution

*The U.S. flag always flies above a state flag.*

Each of the American states, including Colorado, has a state constitution. Colorado's constitution explains how its state government works. It lists the rights and responsibilities of its citizens. It also explains the laws of the state—laws that are particular to Colorado.

The Colorado State Constitution was approved by Colorado voters in 1876. It took effect that same year, when the Territory of Colorado became a state. Since that time, more than 150 **amendments**, or changes, have been made to the original document.

## KNOWLEDGE NUGGET

When the first Colorado Constitution was put to the voters to approve, 15,443 voters out of 19,505 said yes.

In 1876, the population of the Colorado Territory was about 100,000 people.

"We, the people of Colorado, with profound reverence for the Supreme Ruler of the Universe, in order to form a more independent and perfect government; establish justice; insure tranquillity; provide for the common defense; promote the general welfare and secure the blessings of liberty to ourselves and our posterity, do ordain and establish this constitution for the 'State of Colorado'."

Like the U.S. Constitution, the state constitution begins with the people. Its first words are "We, the people of Colorado." This is not just a polite way of beginning the document. It's making the very important point that the state's power and **authority** come from the people themselves. That reminds us that the government, with all its laws, *is* the people. The people themselves make the government what it is by voting and by participating in other ways.

Thirty-nine members of the Colorado constitutional convention gathered on December 20, 1875, to write the new state constitution. It took the delegates 87 days to complete their task.

# CHAPTER 3

# What Is the Government?

## THE CROWN

Some countries have a government called a monarchy. They are ruled by a king or queen who is the head of a royal family.

There are two main types of monarchies. In an absolute monarchy, the king or queen has total power.

In a constitutional monarchy, the king or queen is the head of the state, but his or her power is limited. Laws are made by a parliament of elected officials. The United Kingdom has this sort of monarchy.

The Constitution explains how the government works, but what *is* the government?

When you think of the word government, what do you think of? Maybe you think of the president or the White House. Perhaps you think of adults voting in your school gymnasium or your town's community center. You might hear your parents complaining about having to pay taxes to "the government." Sometimes adults argue about "the government." Other times—for example, at a Memorial Day parade or a baseball game—those same grown-ups may get tears in their eyes when the American flag passes by.

A government is the authority that rules a **society**. Authority is the center, or source, of power. A society is a group of people who live together in a place. It could be a city, a state, or a country. Basically, government is the power

DENVER CAPITOL BUILDING

Curiously, the word "democracy" never appears in the U.S. Constitution.

that rules and protects the people. It's made up of officials who oversee those rules and the people who live according to them. In the United States, there is the **federal** government, which oversees the entire country. Each state also has a state government. The Colorado state government, for example, is concerned only with Colorado.

There are different kinds of governments in various places around the world. In some countries, all governmental power is held by one person or a small group of people. Our government is not like that. Our government is a **democracy**—the power of the government lies in the people themselves.

## THE BRANCHES

Our government is like a tree with three branches: the legislative (lawmaking) branch, the executive (president or governor) branch, and the judicial (justice system) branch. The tree cannot live without all three branches.

# CHAPTER 4

# What Are Rights?

The "I Have a Dream" Monument in Denver's City Park is a tribute to Dr. Martin Luther King Jr. and the civil rights movement of the 1960s.

The word "right" has many meanings. It's a direction: right or left? It's a moral position: right or wrong? "Right" can mean good, fair, correct, appropriate, or accurate. It can also mean agreement, right? Right!

In the constitutional sense, however, "right" means a legal guarantee, or promise, of certain freedoms. A right is something you are allowed to be, allowed to have, or allowed to get. The U.S. Constitution explains citizens' rights in the Bill of Rights. It lists 10 freedoms. One of these is the freedom of speech. This means you can express your opinion, and the government cannot punish you for it. Another right is the freedom of religion. You can belong to the church or faith of your choice or to no church at all. It's the government's job to protect all the freedoms granted by the Constitution.

Colorado law prohibits discrimination in employment, housing, and public places. The law forbids treating people unfairly due to their race, color, national origin, ancestry, sex, sexual orientation, creed, religion, disability, family or marital status, or age.

*Freedom of speech allows citizens to stage public demonstrations like this one in Denver. Here, a group protests certain banking practices.*

There are other sorts of rights. "**Civil rights**" is a term that has to do with social equality. It means treating all people fairly. **Human rights** are rights that all people everywhere deserve simply because they are human beings. These include the right to food, shelter, education, and work. They also include the right to not be abused, to freedom of movement, and the right to life itself. To violate, or go against, those rights means to treat a person as less than human.

The Colorado Civil Rights Commission is the state government agency that enforces Colorado's antidiscrimination laws.

# CHAPTER 5

# Who Is a Citizen?

To be a citizen of Colorado, you must first be a citizen of the United States. According to the U.S. Constitution, citizenship is a birthright. That means every baby born in this country is automatically a citizen.

For people who were not born in the United States, there is another way to become a citizen. Foreigners may apply to the federal government to become "naturalized" citizens. They must meet certain requirements and go through a legal process. Finally, they must take a citizenship test.

> **The Fourteenth Amendment states: "All persons born or naturalized in the United States, and subject to the jurisdiction thereof, are citizens of the United States and of the State wherein they reside."**

Only a "natural born" American citizen may become the president or vice president of the United States.

*A woman in Littleton, Colorado, helps a Korean immigrant learn about American citizenship.*

People who move to Colorado from other states can easily become state citizens. They need to live here for at least six months. They also need to get a state driver's license or Colorado State Identification Card. Children automatically have the same citizenship as their parents. You cannot be a citizen of more than one state at a time.

KNOWLEDGE NUGGET

To become a naturalized citizen, a person must be able to speak, read, and understand the English language.

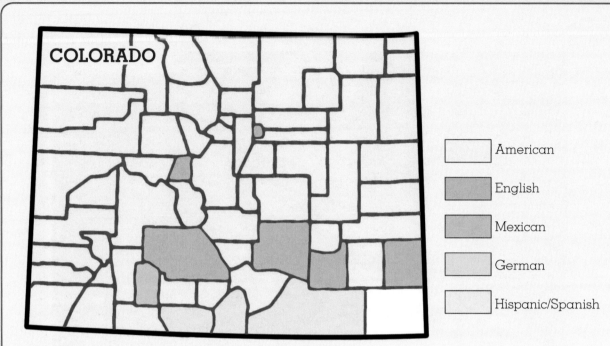

COLORADO

American
English
Mexican
German
Hispanic/Spanish

*The 2000 U.S. census asked residents to name their main ancestry. This map shows the results, by county, for Colorado. German is the most common ancestry, claimed by 22 percent of Coloradans.*

Some people who live in Colorado are not citizens. Perhaps they are visiting for a short while, attending school, or working a temporary job. But some have come to the United States without the government's permission. Usually, they have come to find a better life, but they are here illegally. Those people may be hard workers who contribute in many ways to society, but they are not U.S. citizens. Therefore, they are not citizens of Colorado. They remain citizens of their homeland.

## WHERE DO THEY COME FROM?

In 2013, the top countries of origin for naturalized citizens were Mexico, India, the Philippines, the Dominican Republic, and China.

There are about 180,000 undocumented immigrants living in Colorado. They have come from all over the world, but most have come from Mexico.

*Many people have strong opinions about illegal, or undocumented, immigrants. In two separate demonstrations in Denver, people support (above) or protest against (below) such immigrants.*

## WELCOME, NEW CITIZENS!

Each year, about 680,000 people become naturalized citizens of the United States.

# CHAPTER 6

# The Privilege and Benefits of Citizenship

Being a citizen is a privilege—a special advantage or honor. It's important to know what it means because it's a big part of who you are.

Americans are lucky to live in a place where citizens have rights. In some nations, this is not the case. In some countries, if people don't like what their government is doing, they cannot say so. They might be put in prison. They are not even allowed to leave their country to go live somewhere else.

## KNOWLEDGE NUGGET

Some countries allow dual citizenship. That means a person can be a citizen of more than one country at a time. The United States recognizes, but does not encourage, dual citizenship for its citizens

*Denver area residents plant cherry trees at the Green Valley Ranch recreation center. The trees were donated by Japan to demonstrate the friendship between the United States and Japan.*

Coloradans live in a beautiful state. Its many good citizens make it even better. Citizens can say what they think about the government or anything else. They get to vote for the people who do the work of the government. They can even work for the government themselves if they wish.

Most jobs with federal agencies require U.S. citizenship. Also, it's often necessary to be a U.S. citizen in order to run for elected office.

A FOOD BANK IN COLORADO SPRINGS

## TO THE RESCUE!

Another benefit of U.S. citizenship is international protection. If you encounter trouble when you are out of the country—if you are a victim of a crime or a natural disaster, for example—the U.S. government will help you.

The state provides many services for citizens. For example, Coloradans with low incomes can get help though the Food Assistance Program. This program helps people pay for food. Other state programs help citizens with medical care, college education, and many other things.

People who are not U.S. citizens have rights, too. They may qualify for certain state services, but much depends on whether they are in the United States lawfully.

## FOOD AID NEEDED

One in seven people in Colorado struggles with hunger. That means they might not have enough to eat or that their food is not nutritious enough.

Citizens who want to bring family members to the United States from other countries get priority over those who are not citizens.

A PROUD CITIZEN IN DENVER

# CHAPTER 7

# What Are Citizen Responsibilities?

Citizenship has many benefits. It also has responsibilities. Citizens are expected to perform certain duties. These help society run smoothly. Even kids have responsibilities as citizens.

For example, Coloradans are expected to obey the laws. To obey these rules, a person has to first know what they are. Learning about the law in school is one way kids carry out their citizenship responsibilities. Of course, obeying those laws is another way. Learning about

## AND TO THE REPUBLIC FOR WHICH IT STANDS...

A citizen swears allegiance, or loyalty, to the United States. That's what you are doing when you say the Pledge of Allegiance to the flag.

## VOTING DOWN UNDER

Australia is one of 11 countries that enforce compulsory voting. Australian citizens who do not show up at a polling place to vote may be fined up to $170.

how the government works is also key. In fact, learning all about Colorado is important for all its citizens. That's why you're reading this book right now!

Adult citizens have other responsibilities. Some of them are things people must do. They must pay taxes to the government. They must also keep their driver's license or state identification record up to date. The state needs to know who its citizens are.

Other responsibilities are optional. That means people can do them if they want to. The most important one is voting. Citizens are encouraged to vote, but they are not forced to.

## SHOULD VOTING BE REQUIRED?

Some people think more problems could be solved if more people voted. Nonvoters tend to be young people, have lower incomes, or belong to immigrant or minority groups. Should people be forced to vote? What do you think?

**WHEN DISASTER STRIKES!**
When severe floods devastated Boulder and Larimer Counties in 2013, National Guard units from Colorado and Wyoming rescued more than 2,100 people and 500 pets.

**MEMORIAL DAY SERVICES AT FORT LOGAN NATIONAL CEMETERY IN DENVER.**

One of a citizen's most important responsibilities is to defend the country. Today this responsibility is optional. U.S. soldiers are men and women who chose to join the military. They serve in one of several branches of the U.S. military: the army, navy, marine corps, air force, or coast guard.

At times in the country's past, however, joining the military was not an option. It was required by law for men of certain ages. Under

There are two army bases and four air force bases in Colorado. Altogether, these bases are staffed by about 50,000 military members.

a system called **conscription,** or the *draft*, certain citizens *must* serve in the military. Lawmakers may decide to bring back the draft system if they think it's necessary. Therefore, the federal government gathers information about people living in the country. All male U.S. citizens between the ages of 18 and 25 must register with the Selective Service System. Even noncitizen men between those ages must register.

In addition to an active military, the government maintains reserve forces. These are people who have trained to be soldiers, but are only called upon when they are needed. Until then, they go about their lives.

Each state has its own branch. The Colorado Army National Guard and the Colorado Air National Guard can be called up by the governor if trouble strikes within the state. A weather catastrophe, for example, might leave people without food or water or medical aid. The National Guard can help those people. The Guard can also be called up by the president to serve overseas if necessary.

## FEMALE SOLDIERS

In the past, military women were not allowed to serve in combat. In 2013, that ban was lifted. If conscription is reinstated, should women be drafted? Do you think women should have to register like men do?

The phrase that describes the numbers of people who vote in elections is "voter turnout."

**CHAPTER 8**

# Voting:

## "Of the People, By the People, For the People"

Remember the opening words of the U.S. Constitution? "We the people..." And the first words of the Colorado State Constitution: "We, the people of Colorado..."

We are the people. The people express their will by voting. To vote means to make a choice in an **election**. Everyone's votes are

WE ARE THE PEOPLE

## WORDS TO REMEMBER

In November 1863, President Abraham Lincoln went to Gettysburg, Pennsylvania. At the time, the United States was fighting a terrible Civil War between the Northern states and the Southern states. Just a few months earlier, the war's deadliest battle had taken place in Gettysburg. Lincoln attended a ceremony there to honor the dead soldiers. He gave a short but powerful speech, which became one of the most famous speeches of all time. He talked about what made the United States a great nation. He said our government is "of the people, by the people, [and] for the people."

counted equally, and the choice that gets the most votes wins. This is why voting is one of the most important responsibilities of citizenship. The more people who vote, the better the government works.

In Colorado, all citizens age 18 and older may vote. In some elections, people vote for a **candidate** or several candidates. A candidate is someone who wants to be a government official and is running for election.

WRANGLE UP SOME FACTS

The right to vote is called "suffrage."

### MORE COLORADANS VOTE!
In the 2012 U.S. presidential election, only about 58 percent, or slightly more than half, of all U.S. voters turned out to vote. In Colorado, by contrast, voter turnout was 71 percent.

In some elections, voters consider an **initiative**. That's a suggested new law or a change to an existing law. For example, some citizens of a local school district might ask to raise town taxes in order to pay for new athletic fields at the middle school. In the election, the townspeople can vote for it or against it. This sort of election is called a **referendum**.

*Supporters of an initiative carry signs urging the people of Colorado to vote yes in the upcoming referendum.*

## VOTES FOR WOMEN!

For many years, women were not allowed to vote. Women's groups worked hard to change the law. Finally, on August 18, 1920, the Nineteenth Amendment was ratified. It states, "The right of citizens of the United States to vote shall not be denied or abridged by the United States or by any State on account of sex."

## COLORADO WAS AHEAD OF ITS TIME

In 1893, long before women won the right to vote nationally, women won the right to vote in Colorado. Mrs. John L. Routt, the wife of the first state governor, was the first woman to register to vote.

This photo dates from a 1893 women's suffrage demonstration in Colorado. That same year, women won the right to vote in the state, but not yet in the country.

## IT'S TAX-FREE, TOTO!

In Kansas, you have to pay taxes on a hot-air balloon ride, as long as you stay tethered to the ground. But if you lift off, it's tax-free! Sound silly? It's because tethered rides are considered entertainment and taxed accordingly. Balloons that fly, however, are considered a form of transportation, and therefore not taxed!

Now then, Kansas... what about houses that fly away in tornadoes?

# CHAPTER 9

# Why Pay Taxes?

Nobody likes taxes. People love to complain about them. But most citizens realize that paying taxes is important and necessary.

Tax is money that people and businesses must pay to support the government. This means much more than simply paying the salary of the governor. Taxes pay for all the services the government provides.

TAXES PAY FOR ROAD IMPROVEMENTS

TAXES PAY FOR PUBLIC SCHOOLS

**BIG MONEY**
A state's annual income,
which pays for public expenses,
is called *revenue*.
In 2012, the Colorado tax
revenue came to
$10,250,628,000.

**TAXES PAY FOR FIRE DEPARTMENTS**

State and local taxes pay for public schools, police and fire departments, libraries, roads and highways, and the crews that build and maintain them. (Yes, our taxes even pay the brave folks who plow snowy roads at night during fierce Colorado blizzards!) Federal taxes pay for our country's military and many other things.

Everyone is supposed to pay their fair share of taxes. But figuring out what that share is can be a very complicated matter!

**Taxes are collected in several ways.**

**Income tax**—Workers must pay taxes from their salary, the money they earn at a job, and from other forms of income.

**Sales tax**—This is an extra amount of money added to the price of things you buy. Whether you purchase a candy bar, a car, or a house, you must pay extra money to the government at the time of the sale.

**Property tax**—People who own land, houses, cars, boats, and other kinds of property must pay taxes on those possessions.

## SALES TAX MATH

In Colorado, the state sales tax (as of 2015) is 2.9 percent. That means 2.9 percent of the price of any taxable item is added onto your bill. Many cities in Colorado add additional taxes on top of that.

In Aurora, for example, the total sales tax rate is 7.0 percent. If you buy a bag of dog food for $10.00, you will pay $10.70 at the cash register. Of that 70 cents tax, 29 cents goes to the state government and 41 cents goes to the city government.

# CHAPTER 10

# Obey the Law!

## LEGENDARY OUTLAWS OF THE WILD WEST

Some of the outlaws of the Wild West became legendary. Colorado had its share of bank robbers and stagecoach bandits, but they did not achieve national notoriety like these folks did:

Billy the Kid, Belle Starr, Bill Doolin, Black Bart, the Dalton Brothers, Jesse James, Frank James, William "Curly Bill" Brocius, and Butch Cassidy and the Sundance Kid.

All these bad guys have been the subjects of many books, movies, and TV shows.

Imagine one day your school principal suddenly announces, "Next week is No Rules Week! You can all do exactly what you want and no one will get in trouble, no matter what happens!" Imagine the cheers, the applause, and the squeals of delight!

But wait… before you envision the greatest, happiest, most fun week of your school life, think hard. What might actually happen?

The same is true for society. What would life in Colorado be like without laws? For that answer, we can look to history. Two hundred years ago, this land was part of the American Frontier, sometimes called the Wild West. The word "wild" in the term "Wild West" doesn't refer to wild animals. It means there were no laws. Life on the frontier was dangerous. Gangs of criminals preyed upon pioneer

## THE GOOD GUYS

Not only outlaws earned national reputations. Lawmen were widely admired as well. They included Wyatt Earp, Pat Garrett, Wild Bill Hickok, Bill Tilghman, and Bat Masterson. Masterson spent some of his life in Colorado.

COURTROOM TRIAL

settlements, trains, and stagecoaches. Horse stealing and highway robbery were common. People took **justice** into their own hands, and matters were often settled at the end of a gun.

In short, there was little or no law. Usually the first thing new communities would do as soon as they had enough people was to establish laws and set up a court system.

Societies operate best when laws are fair and people obey them.

A person who takes the law into his or her own hands is a vigilante (vih-juh-LAN-tee). A vigilante acts as a self-appointed police officer, judge, jury—and sometimes executioner—all in one. This is not only dangerous, it's illegal. Vigilantes often work in groups. Why is this kind of activity dangerous? What are some instances of this happening today?

# CHAPTER 11

# You Have a Say

Suppose the Colorado legislature was deciding whether to pass a new law. This law would require boys to wear only blue and girls to wear only pink. What could you, as a citizen of Colorado, do about it? Plenty!

*Colorado Republican State Senator David Balmer votes on a bill, or a new law, during the 2015 Colorado legislative session at the Capitol in Denver.*

Do you think Colorado would ever pass a blue-pink dress code law like the one described here? Why or why not?

*State Senator Abel Tapia discusses an important matter on the floor of the Colorado Senate.*

The state constitution, along with the U.S. Constitution, grants you freedom of expression. That means you have the right to say what you think. Sure, you could just grump to your friends about having to obey this dumb new law. But that wouldn't accomplish much. Freedom of expression is about speaking your mind publicly. There are a number of ways that you can do that. Government works best when citizens play an active role.

### HAVING THEIR SAY
In 2014, more than 1,000 students walked out of their classes at several schools in Jefferson County in Colorado. They were protesting plans to change the way high school U.S. history is taught.

COLLECTING SIGNATURES ON A PETITION

## TELL IT TO THE GOVERNOR

On the Colorado state government website, **www.colorado.gov,** there is a section called "Share Your Opinion." There, you can submit a comment.

Your first job as a citizen is to inform yourself. Get the facts. Forming an opinion based on rumors or lies can be harmful.

Then, you can talk to your government officials. You can meet with them, or you can write a letter or an email. You may also send a letter to the editor of your local newspaper. Newspapers publish letters of opinion about issues that matter to their community. You can hold a public demonstration with others who share your opinion or circulate a **petition**. You can also support an organization devoted to a cause you believe in.

A DEMONSTRATION

# CHAPTER 12

# Debate and Disagreement

What if citizens agreed on all issues, all the time? Life would be very peaceful, but quite dull. Everyone would think the same. Everyone would be the same. The local pizza place would only offer mushroom pizza, because no one would like pepperoni, peppers, onions, or plain cheese. Your opinion wouldn't count because it would be the same as everyone else's. No one's opinion would count.

Of course, pizza preferences are not usually a political issue. And people are obviously not all the same. Folks have different opinions because they have different perspectives, or ways of seeing things. We gain our perspectives from our life experiences—from the people we know, the places we've been, and the things that have happened to us. Not even identical twins have the exact same life experiences!

## WHO, ME?
Before the invention of radio and television, many politicians refused to debate. Presidents didn't debate because they thought it was beneath their dignity. Now, presidential candidates routinely debate several times during an election.

**POINT, COUNTERPOINT**
One way that political candidates explain their ideas to the public is through formal debates. They are an important part of the election process.

*Colorado Senator Mark Udall and Representative Cory Gardner answer questions during a political debate in 2014 in Denver.*

Coloradans come in all ages, races, ethnicities, and genders. They have different religions and political philosophies. By sharing their perspectives, people say, "This is what life is like for me." A wide variety of human experience makes for a more vibrant, interesting, and colorful society. It also makes for a smarter and more tolerant one.

## IN THE SPOTLIGHT

The first televised debate was between John F. Kennedy and Richard Nixon on September 26, 1960. That event is frequently said to have shifted public opinion to Kennedy's favor because Nixon didn't look good on TV. Indeed, Kennedy went on to win the election.

*Candidates for the office of Colorado governor take part in a live, televised debate in 2010 in Aurora. They are, from left, John Hickenlooper, Dan Maes, and Tom Tancredo. Hickenlooper went on to become governor.*

## DEBATE: MARIJUANA

In 2014, Colorado's Amendment 64 legalized the sale of marijuana, or *Cannabis*, for adults 21 and older. Colorado governor John Hickenlooper said he thought that was a mistake. What do you think? Should Colorado voters repeal, or undo, Amendment 64?

Discussion and debate are vital to a democracy. Yes, conflict can lead to arguments and anger. That's part of the democratic process. At its best, though, hashing out differences is a healthy thing. It leads to fresh ideas, creativity, and problem solving. The goal is usually not to force one side to accept the other. The goal, rather, is often to find middle ground, or **compromise**. Sometimes compromise is possible, sometimes it isn't. Either way, listening to others makes a huge difference. Listening with an open mind and open heart leads to understanding—and a stronger, more peaceful society.

### DEBATE: GAY MARRIAGE

In 2006, Colorado voters banned same-sex marriage by passing Amendment 43 to the state constitution. But in 2014, the U.S. 10th Circuit Court of Appeals, which has decision-making power over Colorado, found the ban to be unconstitutional. This undid the amendment and made same-sex marriage legal in the state. What do you think? Did the court make the right decision?

# CHAPTER 13

# How Can Citizens Participate in Their Government?

There are many ways people can participate in their government. The first way is by learning how it works. You can't play basketball if you don't know the rules. You can't play a flute if you don't know the notes. The same is true for playing an active role in your government.

People get excited about presidential elections, but there's more to it than that. Government operates at three levels. The federal government concerns the entire country. (That, of course, is where the president comes in.) The state government concerns itself with your state, in this case, Colorado. Local government concerns itself with your city or town. If you are a Native American living on

"Hail to the Chief" is the official Presidential Anthem of the United States. A military band usually plays the tune when the president appears at a public or official occasion.

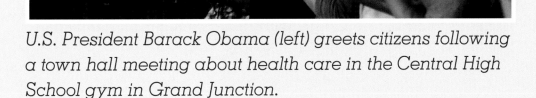

*U.S. President Barack Obama (left) greets citizens following a town hall meeting about health care in the Central High School gym in Grand Junction.*

a reservation, your tribal government is your local government.

Local government often deals with issues closest to the community. Being an active citizen means knowing what's going on in your neighborhood or district. Pay attention. Read the news. Listen to others, and discuss the issues. Even kids can do these things.

In the United States, a person's vote is private and anonymous. You don't put your name to your vote. No one can force you to say how you voted.

In some cases, you might want to attend public meetings. Adult citizens are encouraged to do so. School boards, for example, have public meetings to discuss issues having to do with the local school system.

VOTING

Adult citizens participate in their government by voting. They volunteer for the political party of their choice or even run for office.

You might decide to do the same someday. You might be a future mayor of Aguilar or Durango. You might become a city manager of Grand Junction or a member of the Denver City Council. Are you a future governor of Colorado? Maybe you are our future ... Wait... Do you hear those trumpets and snare drums? Is that "Hail to the Chief" you hear playing? Is it playing for you?

Generally, the more education a person has, the more likely he or she is to vote. Why do you think that is?

There are two main political parties in the United States. Above, Colorado Republicans celebrate an election victory. Below, Senator Mark Udall addresses Colorado Democrats.

# Glossary

**amendment**—a change or an addition to a document, such as the Constitution

**authority**—the power or right to give orders, make decisions, or enforce obedience.

**candidate**—a person who is running for political office

**citizenship**—the status of being a citizen, or a member, of a country, state, city, or town

**civil rights**—the rights of citizens to political and social freedom and equality

**compromise**—an agreement in which each side gives up some, but not all, of what it wants in order to find a solution acceptable to all sides

**conscription**—a system of enforced enlistment in the military

**democracy**—a system of government in which people choose leaders by voting

**election**—the process of choosing by voting

**federal**—relating to the central government of the United States

**government**—the system of people, laws, and officials that conducts the affairs of a country or organization

**human rights**—basic freedoms to which all people are entitled

**initiative**—a proposal for a new law or a change in a law

**justice**—fairness; the process of using laws to judge and punish criminals

**legal**—based on the law

**petition**—a formal written request, typically signed by many people, appealing to an authority regarding a particular cause

**privilege**—a special right or benefit

**referendum**—a process in which a single legal question is presented to the voters for a decision

**rights**—moral or legal entitlements, freedoms, powers, or privileges

**society**—a community or culture of people living together

# Index

## A
amendment(s), 6, 12, 26, 40–41

## B
Bill of Rights, 10

## C
citizen, 4–5, 12–13, 16–17, 19–20, 34, 37, 43

civil rights, 10–11, 27, 40

Colorado State Constitution, 6–7, 24, 35, 40–41

## F
freedom, 10–11, 35

freedom of speech / expression, 10–11, 35

## G
government, 4, 6, 14, 16–18, 21, 23, 25, 28, 31, 35–37, 42–44

governor, 9, 23, 27–28, 36, 40–41, 44

## H
human rights, 11

## I
immigrants, 12–15, 21

## K
kids, 20, 43

## L
laws, 4, 6–8, 10–11, 20, 32–33, 35

## M
military, 22–23, 30, 43

## N
naturalized citizens, 12–15

## P
power, 7–9, 41

president, 8–9, 13, 21, 23, 25, 38, 42–43

## R
responsibilities, 4, 6, 20–22, 25

rights, 4, 6, 10–11, 16, 18, 26, 35

## S
Selective Service System, 23

soldiers, 22–23, 25

## T
taxes, 8, 21, 26, 28–31

## U
U.S. Constitution, 4–5, 7–10, 12, 24, 35

## V
vote / voting, 7–8, 17, 21, 24–27, 43–45

## W
Wild West, 32–33

Due to the changing nature of Internet links, the Rosen Publishing Group, Inc., has developed an online list of websites related to the subject of this book. This site is updated regularly. Please use this link to access the list: www.powerkidslinks.com/soco/poc